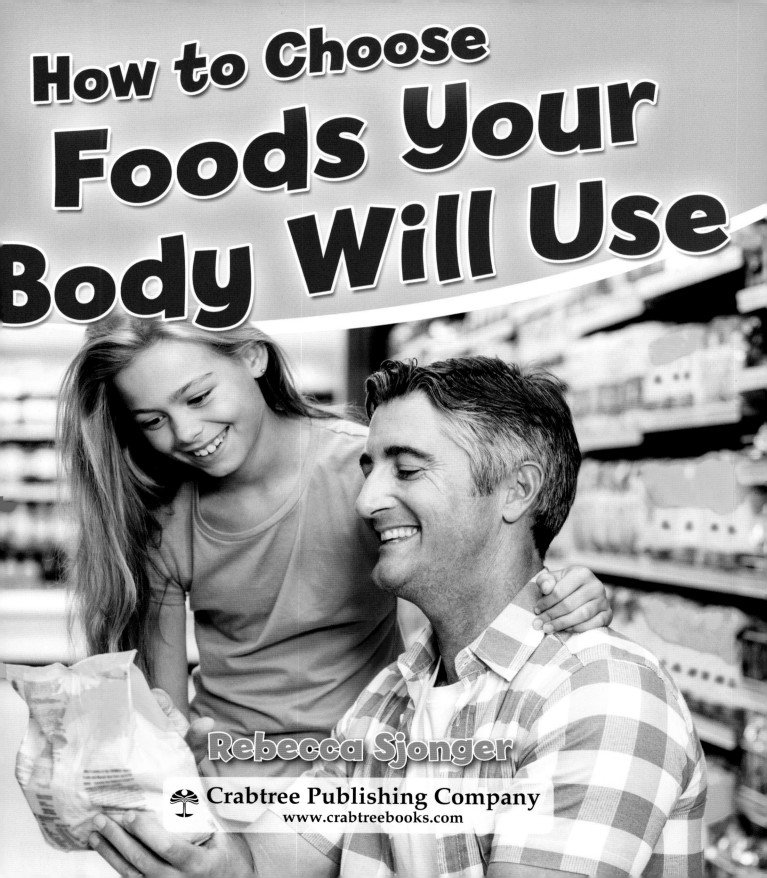

How to Choose
Foods Your
Body Will Use

Rebecca Sjonger

Crabtree Publishing Company
www.crabtreebooks.com

Author
Rebecca Sjonger

Publishing plan research and development
Reagan Miller

Editor
Janine Deschenes

Proofreader
Crystal Sikkens

Consultant
Steve Sanders, Ed.D.,
Professor, Early Childhood Physical Activity,
University of South Florida

Photo research
Tammy McGarr and Crystal Sikkens

Production coordinator and prepress technician
Tammy McGarr

Print coordinator
Margaret Amy Salter

Photographs
iStock: © Rich Legg: p13 (middle right), © JMichl: p14;
© Christopher Futcher: p15; © Susan Chiang: p21 (middle)

All other images by Shutterstock

Library and Archives Canada Cataloguing in Publication

Sjonger, Rebecca, author
How to choose foods your body will use / Rebecca Sjonger.

(Healthy habits for a lifetime)
Includes index.
Issued in print and electronic formats.
ISBN 978-0-7787-2350-9 (bound).--ISBN 978-0-7787-2352-3 (paperback).--
ISBN 978-1-4271-1755-7 (html)

1. Nutrition--Juvenile literature. 2. Diet--Juvenile literature.
3. Health--Juvenile literature. I. Title.

TX355.S5967 2016   j613.2   C2015-907324-3
                                              C2015-907325-1

Library of Congress Cataloging-in-Publication Data

CIP available at the Library of Congress

Crabtree Publishing Company

Printed in Canada/012016/BF20151123

www.crabtreebooks.com   1-800-387-7650

Published in Canada
Crabtree Publishing
616 Welland Ave.
St. Catharines, Ontario
L2M 5V6

Published in the United States
Crabtree Publishing
PMB 59051
350 Fifth Avenue, 59th Floor
New York, New York 10118

Published in the United Kingdom
Crabtree Publishing
Maritime House
Basin Road North, Hove
BN41 1WR

Published in Australia
Crabtree Publishing
3 Charles Street
Coburg North
VIC 3058

Contents

Healthy habits

What do you think the **habits** below have in common?

- ✔ **Being active for 60 minutes every day**
- ✔ **Dealing well with stress**
- ✔ **Getting 10 hours of sleep each night**
- ✔ **Choosing** nutritious **foods and drinks**

They are all part of being healthy for a lifetime!

Anyone can form healthy habits. Get started today!

Forming healthy habits is easier when you choose foods your body will use. Nutritious foods and drinks give you **energy**. They also help your muscles, bones, and teeth grow properly. Choosing foods that are good for your body is good for your brain, too. You will focus and remember what you learn at school better. Eating well even helps you to live longer.

Whole foods

Whole foods are in their most natural and nutritious forms. Peanuts in shells are whole foods. They grow on plants. Plants give us many whole foods. Apples and other fruits grow out of a plant's flowers. Dried seeds become **grains**, such as rice. Did you know that lettuces are leaves? We even eat plant roots, such as carrots!

apple trees

rice plants

Whole foods and drinks also come from birds, fish, and **mammals**. Meat, seafood, and eggs are all sources of **protein**. The milk from some animals gives us **dairy** foods.

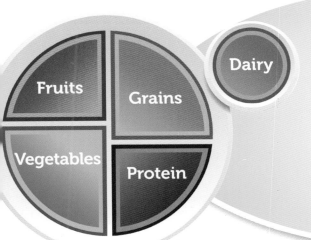

Whole peanuts look the same as they did when farmers took them out of the ground.

Foods are put into five groups based on their sources or **nutrients**:

1. Fruits
2. Vegetables
3. Grains
4. Plant and animal proteins
5. Dairy

Fruits

Grains

Dairy

Vegetables

Protein

Processed foods

Processed foods are created when whole foods are changed from their natural forms. Processed foods often have added **ingredients**. These may help foods last longer. They may also change the taste of foods. Added ingredients often make foods less healthy to eat.

Nutrition Facts

Serving size	About 38 pieces	Serving per Container	16
Amount per serving		Calories	130

		% Daily Value*
		11%
Total fat	7 g	3%
Saturated fat	0.5 g	0%
Cholesterol	0 mg	10%
Sodium	250 mg	5%
Total carbohydrate	16 g	2%
Dietary Fiber	Less than 1 g	
Sugar	Less than 1 g	
Protein	Less than 1 g	

Vitamin A	0%	Vitamin C	2%
Calcium	0%	Iron	2%

Based on 2,000 calories / day

Packages can make foods and drinks appear good for you when they are not. Always check the ingredients. Most "veggie" chips are as bad for you as regular potato chips. Snack on your favorite crunchy vegetables instead!

For example, shelled and roasted peanuts are processed. Added flavors such as salt make them less healthy for you. Another process crushes the nuts into peanut butter. A small jar of peanut butter contains 500 peanuts. It also has a lot of added sugar and salt. Whole peanuts are a much healthier option.

Frozen vegetables with no added ingredients are often as good for you as the fresh forms.

Junk foods

Eating a lot of junk foods and fast food restaurant meals harms your health. They contain few nutrients. All they have to offer are unhealthy amounts of salt, sugar, and solid fats. They may also include many unnatural ingredients.

Junk foods do not help your body. Instead, choose foods and drinks your body can use!

The ways junk foods are prepared may also be bad for your health. For example, restaurants cook french fries in large tanks of oil. This soaks them in unhealthy fats.

One **serving** of soda may contain over six teaspoons (30 ml) of sugar. That is more sugar than anyone should have in a whole day! Make it a habit to drink water instead of sugary drinks.

11

Energy in, energy out

Foods and drinks contain units of energy called **calories**. Your body needs this energy. About half of it goes toward basic tasks such as breathing and growing. Your body uses the rest to keep it moving. Our bodies change any unused calories into body fat. The extra fat causes people to gain weight.

Excerise helps burn off unused calories.

Aim to take in your calories from foods and drinks that are rich in nutrients. Junk foods are high in calories, but low in nutrients.

Different foods contain different amounts of calories.

Check out these examples of foods that contain about 100 calories and activities that use about 100 calories.

Energy In

100 raspberries
1/3 of a cheeseburger
28 baby carrots
10 salted potato chips
small granola bar

Energy Out

swimming laps (30 minutes)
biking (35 minutes)
playing tag (45 minutes)
bowling (one hour)
playing Frisbee (two hours)

Meals and Snacks

Hunger is your body's way of telling you that it needs more energy. Try to take in most of your nutrients and calories during meals. Choose tasty, nutritious snacks if you get hungry between meals. Grab a banana, whole-grain crackers, yogurt, or a handful of nuts.

Eat slowly and enjoy your food. Rushing through your meals and snacks can cause you to overeat. You should stop eating if your stomach feels full, even if there is still food on your plate.

Breakfast is the first and most important meal of the day. Your brain and body cannot work properly if you skip breakfast. You may also be tempted to snack on junk foods to get a quick boost of energy.

Mix it up!

It is important to choose nutritious foods and drinks throughout the day, not just for one meal or snack. Aim to eat a variety of foods that are prepared in different ways. This will help you get a wide range of nutrients each day. Whenever you can, choose foods that your body can use. Cut down on junk foods and sugary drinks.

Are there nutritious foods you do not like to eat? Ask yourself why. Is it the texture, smell, look, or flavor? Find out if there are different ways to prepare or eat that food. Make it your goal to check out new foods. Ask a friend from a different culture what his or her favorite foods are. Then give them a try!

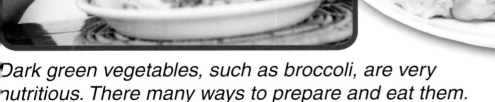

Dark green vegetables, such as broccoli, are very nutritious. There many ways to prepare and eat them.

17

Tasty tips

Sign up for a fun cooking class for kids. You will learn basic skills such as following recipes and using kitchen equipment safely.

Do you usually eat in front of the TV? Switch it up and sit at the table for your next meal. You will enjoy your food more when you pay closer attention to it.

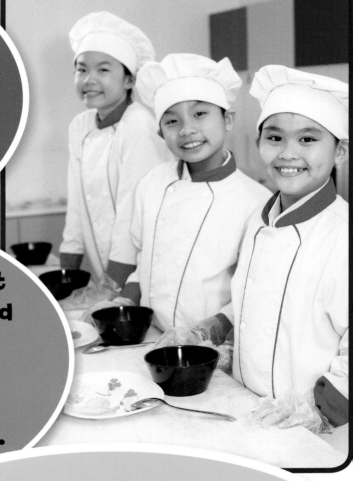

Watch what you add! Jams, ketchup, and salad dressings all contain calories. They also have extra sugar, salt, and fat.

Ask a parent to help you check the serving sizes on packaged foods and drinks. A container that looks like it is for one person may hold multiple servings.

People who do not eat foods that come from animals can get protein from many plant-based foods, such as quinoa, beans, and nuts.

Look for juices labeled "100% pure." They are the healthiest choices because there are no added ingredients.

What's for dinner?

Are you ready for a healthy eating challenge?
Follow these steps to make dinner for your family!

1 Begin by choosing a nutritious dinner to make. You could ask a parent to help you find a simple recipe that your family loves to eat. You could also look for recipes in cookbooks for kids. Pick a healthy side dish, such as a tossed salad or raw vegetables. Decide which drinks you will serve with your dinner.

2 Write a shopping list. Then go to a grocery store with a parent to buy the food you need for your meal.

3 Note how the food is stored when you unload your groceries at home. What goes in the fridge, in the freezer, or in a cupboard?

4 Assist with preparing the meal as much as possible. Ask if you can help with tasks such as:
- measuring foods
- rinsing vegetables or grains
- using tools such as a grater, can opener, or blender
- stirring and scooping
- tossing together ingredients

5 Choose which dishes, utensils, serving pieces, and glasses you will need.

6 Set a place at the table for each member of your family.

7 Serve your dinner and enjoy!

Show what you know!

1. Which of the following is a plant-based food?

   a. Eggs

   b. Apples

   c. Fish

   d. Milk

2. What is a calorie?

   a. Energy a body needs to work properly

   b. Something a body stores as fat

   c. A unit for measuring energy

   d. All of the above

3. Which of the following is a whole food or drink?

   a. Soda

   b. Chocolate bar

   c. Peanuts in shells

   d. Pizza

4. Why should you eat a variety of foods?

   a. To get a variety of nutrients

   b. To narrow down one favorite to eat

   c. To choose the tastiest junk foods

   d. None of the above

Answers: 1. b; 2. d; 3. c; 4. a

Learning more

Websites

Recipes for kids, including ideas for people with special diets
http://kidshealth.org/kid/recipes

Fun games to learn more about nutrition and healthy eating
http://www.healthyeating.org/Healthy-Kids/Kids-Games-Activities.aspx

Information on eating healthy and physical activity
https://kids.usa.gov/exercise-and-eating-healthy

Everything you need to know about food labels
http://pbskids.org/itsmylife/body/foodsmarts/article4.html

Books

Gleisner, Jenna Lee. *My Body Needs Food*. Amicus, 2014.

Knighton, Kate. *Why Shouldn't I Eat Junk Food?* Usborne, 2015.

Kreisman, Rachelle. *You Want Me to Eat That? A Kids' Guide to Eating Right*. Lerner, 2014.

Sjonger, Rebecca. *On a Mission for Good Nutrition!* Crabtree, 2015.

Most websites with addresses that end in ".org" or ".gov" have current information that you can trust.

Words to know

calorie [CAH-le-ree] noun A unit of measurement related to food energy

dairy [DARE-ee] noun A group of foods and drinks that are made from animal milk

energy [en-ER-gee] noun The body or mind's ability to do work

grains [GRANE] noun A group of foods made from the dried seeds of grass-like plants

habit [HAB-it] noun A way someone usually acts or thinks

ingredient [in-GREE-dee-ent] noun One part of a food

mammal [MA-mel] noun A kind of animal that is covered in hair or fur and feeds milk to its babies

nutrient [NEW-tree-ent] noun Something tha is found in foods that a body needs to functio

nutritious [NEW-trish-ush] adjective Describes a food or drink that provides nutrients

processed [PRO-ses-d] adjective Describes a food that has been changed from its natura state

protein [PRO-teen] noun A nutrient the body needs to function

serving [SIR-ving] noun An amount of drink or food consumed at one time

A noun is a person, place, or thing. An adjective tells us what something is like.

Index

24